PERFECT PETS

Susan Schafer

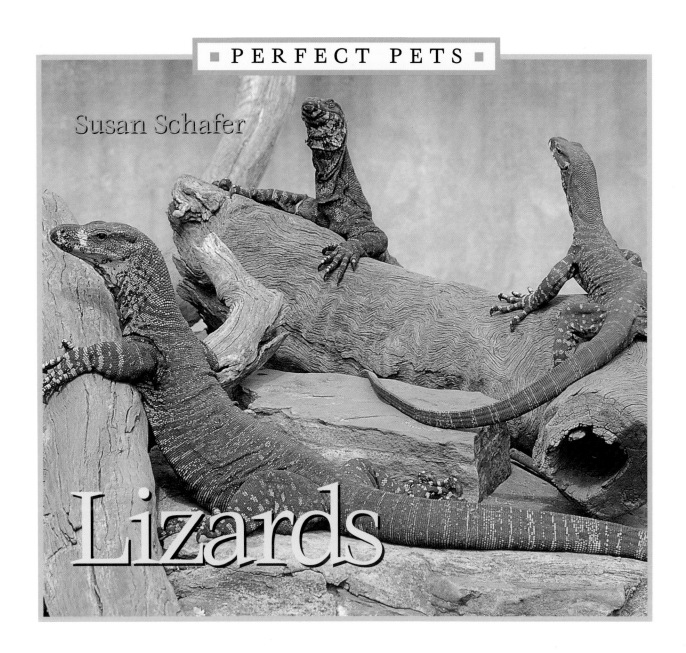

Lizards

BENCHMARK BOOKS

MARSHALL CAVENDISH
NEW YORK

With special thanks to the people who care
about lizards

Benchmark Books
Marshall Cavendish Corporation
99 White Plains Road
Tarrytown, New York 10591

© 2001 Marshall Cavendish Corporation

Library of Congress Cataloging-in-Publication Data
Schafer, Susan, date.
Lizards / Susan Schafer.
p.   cm. — (Perfect Pets)
Includes bibliographical references (p.   ) and index.
Summary: Describes various kinds of lizards while focusing
on those which could best serve as pets by indicating the food
they need and the care they require.
ISBN 0-7614-1103-8 (lb)
1. Lizards as pets—Juvenile literature. [1. Lizards as pets. 2.
Pets.] I. Title. II. Series.
SF459.L5 S32   2001   639.3'95 dc21   99-058088   CIP   AC

Photo research by Candlepants, Inc.

Cover photo: *Dennis Sheridan*
Back cover photo: *A. B. Sheldon Nature Photography*

The photographs in this book are used by permission and
through the courtesy of: *A. B. Sheldon Nature Photography*: 1,
19. *Animals Animals*: Stephen Dalton, 12; Zig Leszczynski, 20;
Robert Pearcy, 25, 30. *Corbis-Bettman*: Richard T. Nowitz, 8.
Dennis Sheridan: 6, 9, 10, 11, 13, 15 (top), 15 (bottom), 16, 22, 23, 29.
Norvia Behling: 26. *Photo Researchers, Inc*: T. McHugh, title
page, 14 (left); Gregory G. Dimijian, 4; John Dommzas, 21;
Lawrence Migdale, 28. *Susan Schafer*: 3, 14 (right), 18, 19, 27.

Printed in Hong Kong
6   5   4   3   2   1

In Memory of Aussie,
who loved the little blue-bellies

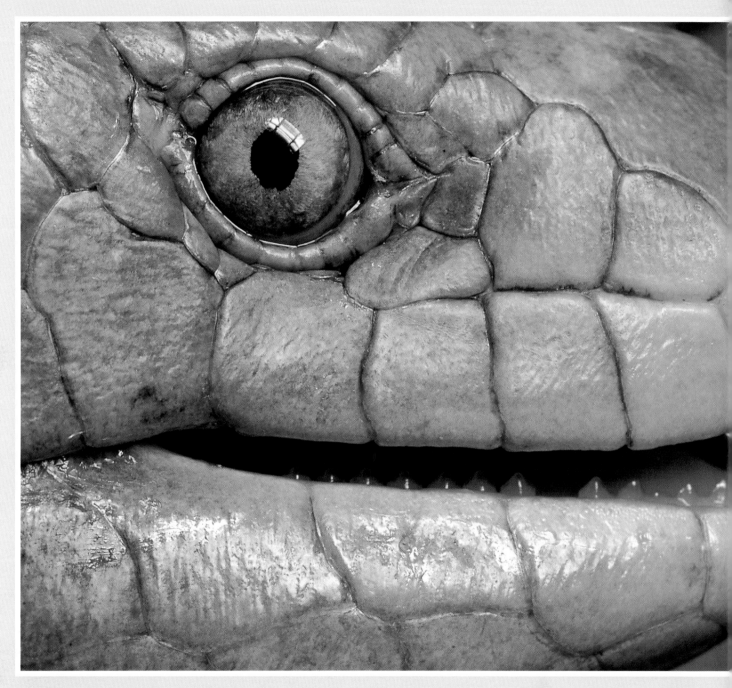

The lizards of today, like this Solomon Island skink, are perfect miniatures of the sharp-eyed, scaly dinosaurs of the prehistoric past.

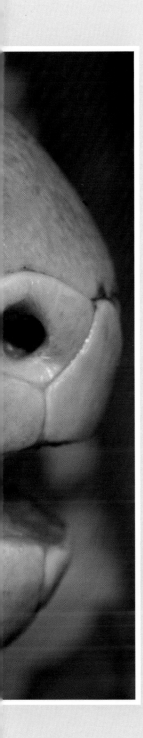

Imagine

a time more than a hundred million years ago. A scaly creature crashes through the jungle brush. Sharp claws extend from toes at the ends of powerful legs and feet. Pointed teeth glisten within powerful jaws. Do you see a dinosaur? A fierce *Tyrannosaurus rex* with sparkling eyes? Or a massive *Allosaurus* on the lookout for prey?

No, it is not a giant of the day, but a miniature version of the dinosaur. Yet this seemingly unimportant little guy would end up beating out even the greatest of the dinosaurs. Its relatives would survive to become the most successful group of reptiles living in the world today—the lizards.

Think of just about anyplace on Earth, and some sort of lizard lives there. Lizards live in deserts, forests, swamps, and mountains. They live where it is hot and where it is cold. In each place, they survive in their own special way. Some climb up rocks, trees, and bushes. Some burrow underground or swim in ponds and rivers. Others live on the ocean shore. A few even live in people's houses.

Wherever lizards live, people are superstitious about them. In the southern part of the United States, the glass lizard got its name because it seems to break into pieces when disturbed. Some people believe that it can rejoin the pieces later, but it's not true. Like other lizards, it can lose its tail when grabbed. Sometimes the tail breaks into more than one piece. The tail will not reattach, but a new one will eventually grow back.

Many people think that the bite of a lizard, such as a blue-belly or a gecko, is poisonous. But the Gila monster and the beaded lizard are the only poisonous lizards in the world. These large, **terrestrial** lizards live in the deserts of the southwestern United

In spite of being a fierce predator, Velociraptor, *which means "swift robber," was lost to Earth about 80 million years ago.*

An artist paints a dragon's head that will decorate the bow of a boat during a Chinese dragon-boat ceremony.

States and Mexico, but they are shy and rarely bite people. In spite of this, many people are afraid of lizards and try to get rid of them. Around the world, lizards are killed every day because of this fear.

Not all people treat lizards unkindly. Most know that they are helpful because they eat the insects that invade our gardens. Others believe that lizards bring good luck. In some parts of Asia, the owners of a newly-built house wait to hear the call of a tokay gecko. They believe that the sooner they hear the call, the luckier they will be in their new home. Still others believe that if the gecko barks when a baby is born, it is a sign that the child will live a happy life.

Long ago, people in China believed that dragons could change themselves into lizards and bring the rain. After the rains, the dragon would stretch itself across the sky and appear as a rainbow. The dragon lizard is still honored every year in southern China, where the people hold a dragon-boat ceremony.

The venom of the beaded lizard drains into its mouth from bulging glands on the sides of its head. It can't inject its venom like a snake, but must hold onto its prey until the venom works.

9

Day geckos seem to sparkle like jewels. Their bright green body may be decorated with blue, red or yellow spots, dashes, or stripes.

Would

you recognize a lizard if you saw one? Would you see spiny scales, a long tail, and four legs? You might picture a blue-belly that sits in the sun and bobs its head up and down. Or a Komodo dragon, as long as a car and as fierce as a tiger. Or an alien-looking chameleon that changes colors and swivels its eyes like tiny telescopes.

Not all lizards are scaly and have four legs. Many skinks are as smooth as a polished table. And some lizards, like the glass lizards, have no legs at all! They look like long snakes on the outside, but inside they still have the bone structure of a lizard. Legless lizards burrow through soil, grass, and leaves.

One way of knowing if a legless reptile is a lizard or a snake

Most skinks, like these blue-tailed skinks, are smooth and glossy. Predators are attracted to the bright blue tail, which breaks off and allows the skink to escape.

Long toes and sharp claws help lizards grasp branches and rocks.

A Toe For Every Occasion

Depending on where a lizard lives, it has special toes to help it survive. Some lizards have strong fingers and sharp claws for digging or tearing. Others have flat, clinging toes for climbing trees. Some have webbed toes for swimming in water or walking on soft sand. And a few—those that burrow through the ground or the leaves on the forest floor—have no toes at all, because they have no legs to put them on!

is to look closely at its eyes (if it's safe to do so). Lizards without legs always have eyelids that blink. Snakes can't blink their eyes.

Lizards come in all sizes and shapes, but large or small, long or short, most are quick and agile. They are the athletes of the reptile world. They can run like Olympic sprinters, leap like basketball players, and shimmy up cliffs better than the world's top rock climbers. A few, such as the flying dragons, can sail through the air as gracefully as hang gliders.

Arboreal lizards such as the Mexican green iguana have strong legs with grasping toes and sharp claws to help them hold onto trees. Chameleons have an "extra" hand that any football player would envy. If their feet are busy, they simply grab on with their tail.

With their long bodies and forked tongues, monitor lizards look like storybook dragons. Some are as small as a ruler. Others, such as the Nile monitor, can be longer than most men are tall. *Whaaack!* Like hockey players smacking a puck with their sticks, monitor lizards defend themselves against enemies using their long, muscular tails. If that doesn't work, they bite with hundreds of sharp, slicing teeth.

Many lizards could make the swim team. The Galapagos

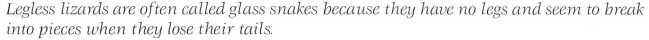

Legless lizards are often called glass snakes because they have no legs and seem to break into pieces when they lose their tails.

Leopard geckos have sharp, catlike eyes that help them spot and catch insects, even at night.

If danger threatens, an arboreal lizard can run straight up the trunk of a tree.

marine iguana dives through the surf and swims to the ocean floor to graze on seaweed. Australian water dragons and Asian water monitors swim like Olympic competitors, but Indonesian Komodo dragons are the real marathon swimmers. They swim for miles in the ocean to get from island to island. North American fringe-toed lizards can even swim through sand! Imagine that the next time you're at the beach.

The basilisk, a lizard from Central America, is so speedy that it can run on water. The fringes on its toes act like water skis to keep it from sinking. The best water polo players can't beat that!

While most lizards are athletic and swift, the Gila monster is stocky and slow. It relies on a bulldog-like bite for its protection.

Named for a legendary reptile whose stare and breath could kill, the basilisk lizard would rather run away than attack when danger threatens.

Chameleons change color to signal their moods. They are brightly colored when they feel aggressive, warm, or happy. They are dark when they feel threatened, cold, or sick.

Lizards

belong to special families, depending on the kinds of scales and bones they have. Green iguanas, anoles, blue-bellies, and chuckwallas belong to the iguana family. To protect themselves, green iguanas and anoles hide in trees. Blue-bellies dive into holes. Chuckwallas squeeze themselves between rocks, suck in air, and blow themselves up like balloons so they can't be pried out by a **predator**.

Chameleons, skinks, and geckos each belong to their own families. The savannah monitor and Komodo dragon belong to the monitor family. Australian water dragons and bearded dragons belong to the agama family. When frightened, water dragons dive into rivers and hide underwater. Like peacocks fanning their tails, bearded dragons spread spiny beards around their heads. This trick makes them look bigger than they really are.

The Big Bluff

Lizards may try to bluff their way out of danger. Many try to look ferocious by opening their mouths wide or by hissing. Some stick out their tongues. Others fold out a spiny beard. One even blows itself up like a balloon to make it look bigger and scarier than it really is.

Trying to look big and fierce, a bearded dragon gapes its mouth and spreads its spiny beard.

There are more lizards in the world today—about 3,000 kinds—than any other kind of reptile. They live in so many special ways that it would take a huge book to describe them all, but of all the lizards, only a few make good pets. That means that only a few will adapt well to **captivity**.

One of these is the green iguana. With its spiny back and **dewlap** hanging from its throat, it looks a dinosaur. The dewlap acts like a flag to send signals to other green iguanas. Blue-bellies also make good pets.

Geckos are popular because they are unique. Most lizards are silent, but geckos have voices. Each type has its own special call, from a soft chirp to a startling scream. Geckos use their voices to call their mates.

Other geckos, such as the house gecko, have special hair-like cells on their toes that can cling to the tiniest cracks.

The savannah monitor is one of the few lizards that adapts well to captivity. Still, it needs to bask regularly in natural sunlight.

The Tokay gecko has clinging toes that allow it to climb up walls. It got its name from the sound it makes: "toe-kay!"

They can scoot up smooth walls, across windows, and can even run upside-down on a ceiling!

Of all the geckos, the Asian leopard gecko makes the best pet. Geckos are delicate, however, and must be handled carefully. Their soft skin tears easily, and, like other lizards, their tail falls off if grabbed.

If you like skinks, western skinks and Mediterranean-eyed skinks make good pets. Blue-tongued skinks and monitor lizards are popular, but they are large, active, and need a lot of natural sunlight. Many people want an African chameleon for a pet, but they are not a good choice. They are tricky to care for and die easily.

Whichever lizard you choose, you must learn as much as you can about it *before* you bring it home. If you don't, you will be risking its life. Lizards are already disappearing from the

Flag-Waving, Head-Bobbing Hellos

Most lizards do not have a voice, but that doesn't stop them from "talking" to each other. Each kind of lizard has its own special way of sending messages to the other lizards around it. Many have a brightly colored flap of skin on their neck that they can stick out like a flag. Other lizards bob their heads up and down, nodding out their own special form of Morse code. Some lizards wave their arms at each other. Others change colors from dull to bright green, red, yellow, or blue.

Green iguanas "talk" to one another by bobbing their heads and sticking out the large flaps of skin, called dewlaps, under their throats.

earth. Many are rare or **endangered**. If you care about lizards, you will never take one from its natural **habitat** or buy one that came from the wild. Find out from a reptile society or **herpetology** club in your area where to get a lizard born in captivity. Captive-bred lizards live longer than wild-caught lizards. Your special pet will be healthier, and you will be helping to conserve nature.

Because their skin can rip and their tail can fall off, geckos must be handled carefully.

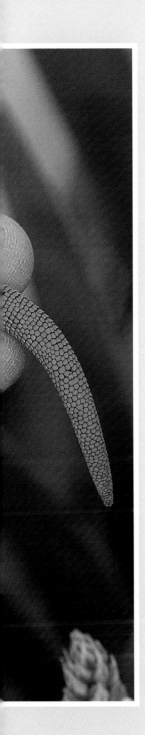

To get ready

for your special pet, buy or make a roomy cage. One side of the cage should be cool (around 72-76°F/22-24°C). The other side should be warm (around 84-86°F/29-30°C). Your lizard will move in and out of the heat to keep its temperature just right.

Use a heat lamp or hot rock to make a "hot spot" on the warm side of the cage. The hot spot should never get hotter than 88°F (31°C). Make sure your lizard can't burn itself on the heat lamp. Turn off the hot spot at night, but make sure the cage temperature does not drop below 65°F (18°C). If your lizard is active, eating well, and gaining weight, then you probably have the temperature right.

To build strong bones, lizards need natural sunlight. They need

Lizards need the sun or a heat lamp to warm themselves. If they cannot keep their body at the right temperature, they will become ill.

an outdoor cage with places to bask in the sun and places to hide in the cool shade. Never put a lizard outside in a glass or plastic cage. The heat will build up and kill it. Make the cage out of screen so air can circulate. On sunny days, lizards should spend at least an hour outside.

Cover the bottom of your lizard's cage with potting soil, peat moss, or alfalfa pellets. Never use sand, gravel, kitty litter, ground corncobs, perlite, or wood shavings. Your lizard might get sick if it eats some. Change the soil whenever it is spoiled or sour.

Give your lizard a "hide box" to crawl into at night. The box should be a little bigger than the lizard itself, well insulated, and dry. You can buy one, make one, or use a cardboard box. Garden pots broken in half and rounded pieces of bark work well, too.

Arboreal lizards, such as the green iguana, need branches to climb on. Terrestrial lizards, such as blue-bellies, like rocks. Make sure they will not collapse and crush your lizard.

Most lizards don't like to be held, so give them an interesting place to live, and you can enjoy watching them explore their home. They might hide at first, but once they get used to you, they will stay out.

You can keep a lizard by itself. It won't get lonely. If you have more, make sure that only one is a male. Males fight over food, shelter, hot spots, and females. If one lizard gets hurt, turns a sickly gray, or stops basking or eating, it needs to be in a cage by itself.

Keeping two different sizes of lizards together can sometimes be risky. The larger one might eat the smaller one.

Always have clean, fresh water for your lizard to drink. Make sure the water is shallow so your lizard doesn't drown. If you have a large pond, make sure it has steps so your pet can climb out.

Lizards need a variety of foods. Those that eat fruits, flowers, and vegetables are attracted to red and yellow colors. Those that eat insects, earthworms, and small animals are attracted by movement. Be careful when feeding large lizards like blue-tongued skinks and monitors. Your wiggling fingers might look like a meal to them!

Offer food to your lizard every day, even if it doesn't eat. It needs to be warmed up first. If its body is cold, it will not be able to digest its food. During cold weather, it may not eat as much or as often.

Weigh your lizard regularly. If it stays the same weight or gains weight, it is probably healthy. If it loses weight or has a bubbly nose, weepy eyes, or gums covered with a soft, cheesy material, it needs to see a **veterinarian** who treats reptiles.

Some lizards, such as the leopard gecko and blue-tongued skink, overeat in captivity. Their muscles should be full and rounded, but if they are bulging with fat, cut back on their food.

Adult green iguanas are **herbivores**. Feed them collards,

The best way to keep track of a lizard's health is to weigh it. Over time, its weight should stay the same or increase.

Tiger of the Lizard World

The largest lizard in the world is the Komodo dragon, found on just a few islands in Indonesia. If it stretched out on a couch, its head and tail would stick out over the ends. A powerful hunter, it can bring down a water buffalo and swallow a deer whole.

Few animals are safe from a predator as fierce and powerful as the Komodo dragon.

Variety is the key to health, so offer your lizard several different kinds of food. And don't forget to add the vitamins!

dandelion greens, broccoli, shredded carrots, Brussels sprouts, string beans, and grass. Because they are poisonous to reptiles, never feed them spinach, rhubarb leaves, beets, or cauliflower.

Mix a little chopped fruit with the vegetables. Try apples, grapes, peaches, pears, plums, papayas, and strawberries. Young green iguanas eat insects as well as vegetables and fruits.

Sprinkle vitamins on your lizard's food every day. Mix half

a cup of powdered calcium carbonate (available at pharmacies) with half a cup of powdered vitamins made especially for reptiles.

Leopard geckos, blue-bellies, and small skinks are **insectivores**. Offer them crickets, waxworms, mealworms, silkworms, and grasshoppers. To slow down the insects, put them in the refrigerator for about ten minutes. Coat the insects with the calcium and vitamin mixture by shaking them together in a plastic jar or paper bag.

Monitor lizards are **carnivores**. Feed them mice, rats, and occasionally fish. The fish must be fresh and whole. Frozen, thawed fish is missing important vitamins. Never give a lizard dog food, cat food, or raw meat or it may get sick.

With your help, your lizard will live a long, healthy life. It will be a survivor, just like its ancestors who outlived the dinosaurs to succeed in the modern world.

Carnivores and insectivores like this worm-munching crocodile lizard need fresh, whole animals to eat.

Fun Facts

- One of the smallest lizards is a type of gecko. At its biggest, it could easily curl itself up on top of a quarter.

- The flying dragon of Asia has large flaps of skin attached to its ribs. When it flattens itself out, its sides become wings. Jumping into the air, it then glides from tree to tree.

- In the deserts of the southwestern United States, the horned lizard startles its predators by squirting blood from the corners of its eyes.

- The chameleon catches its food by shooting its tongue out of its mouth like a harpoon. The tongue reaches farther than the length of the lizard's body.

- The endangered Gila monster and its close relative, the Mexican beaded lizard, are the only two venomous lizards in the world.

- Almost all of the "snakes" in the tomb scene of "Raiders of the Lost Ark," where Indiana Jones discovers the Ark of the Covenant, were actually legless lizards called European glass lizards.

Glossary

arboreal: Living in trees.

captivity: The condition of being caught and held in a confined area such as a cage.

carnivore: An animal that eats other animals.

dewlap: A flap of skin hanging from under the throat.

endangered: In danger of disappearing from Earth.

habitat: The area or kind of environment in which an animal normally lives.

herbivore: An animal that eats plants.

herpetology: The scientific study of reptiles and amphibians.

insectivore: An animal that eats insects.

predator: An animal that lives by killing and eating other animals.

terrestrial: Living on land.

veterinarian: A doctor who takes care of animals.

Find Out More About Lizards

Call the reptile department of a local zoo and ask for the name of the herpetology club nearest you.

Visit the Web site *www.sonic.net/~melissk/society.html#societies* for a list of reptile societies in your area, or search the Internet using the words "herpetological society."

Cogger, Harold G., and Richard G. Zweifel, Eds. *Reptiles & Amphibians.* New York: Smithmark Publishers, 1992.

Mattison, Chris. *The Care of Reptiles and Amphibians in Captivity.* London: Blandford Press, 1987.

Obst, Fritz Jurgen, Klaus Richter, and Udo Jacob. *The Completely Illustrated Atlas of Reptiles and Amphibians for the Terrarium.* Neptune City, NJ: T.F.H. Publications, 1988.

Schafer, Susan. *The Komodo Dragon.* New York: Dillon Press, Macmillan Publishing Company, 1992.

Index

About the Author

Susan Schafer's study of reptiles has taken her around the world, from the deserts of North America to the forests of South America, Australia, and New Zealand. *Turtles* was her first book in the *Perfect Pets* series. She has also written books for children about the Galapagos tortoise, the Komodo dragon, and the vulture. She lives on a ranch outside San Luis Obispo, California, with her husband, horses, and dogs, and enjoys watching the blue-bellies that scamper around on the deck of her home.